THE VIKINGS

ANNE PEARSON

Viking
C.1

Acknowledgments

The publishers would like to thank Dr. Richard Hall of the York Archaeological Trust for his invaluable assistance and advice during the preparation of this book; Bill Le Fever, who illustrated the see-through pages and jacket; and the organizations which have given their permission to reproduce the following pictures:

The British Library: 45 top left. **Peter Clayton:** 27 bottom, 44 top
Published by permission of the Danish National Museum, Copenhagen: 10 top, 21 center left, 22 top, 22 center left, 34 bottom left
Werner Forman Archive: 24 top left, 40 top left
Werner Forman\National Museum, Copenhagen: 22 bottom left, 40 bottom
Werner Forman\Statens Historiska Museum, Stockholm: 4 bottom, 38 bottom
Werner Forman\University Museum of National Antiquities, Uppsala: 26 top
Werner Forman\Upplandsmuseet, Uppsala: 4 top. **Gotlands Fornsal:** 20 top
Historisk Museum - Universitetet I Bergen: 18 top, 20 bottom
Michael Holford\British Museum: 14 top
Michael Holford\Guildhall Museum: 22 bottom center
Michael Holford\Statens Historiska Museum, Stockholm: 21 top center, 21 bottom right, 24 top right, 42 top left
Knudsens Fotosenter: 7 bottom, 9 bottom, 24 top right, 30 top left, 32 bottom
Kunglige Biblioteket (The Royal Library), Stockholm: 29 bottom
The National Museum of Ireland: 22 bottom right
The Restoration Workshop of Nidaros Cathedral: 7 top
Parks Canada, Canadian Heritage\G Vandervloogt: 34 top
Photoresources\C M Dixon: 21 top left, top center, bottom left
Royal Coin Cabinet, Stockholm: 16 top, 27 right
York Archaeological Trust Historical Picture Library: 8 top, 12 top, 21 top right, 42 top right

Illustrators:
Richard Berridge: 6, 8, 9, 15, 42, 43, 44, 45. **Richard Draper:** 40
Bill Le Fever: 17, 25, 33, 41. **James Field:** 10-11, 11, 24, 28-29
Philip Hood: 26, 27, 36. **Nigel Longden:** 23, 30, 31
Kevin Maddison: 4-5. **Finbarr O'Connor:** 32, 38, 39, 46-47
Chris Orr: 16, 20, 21. **Tony Randall:** 12, 13, 14, 18, 19, 34, 35, 37

VIKING
Published by the Penguin Group
Penguin Books USA Inc., 375 Hudson Street, New York, New York 10014, U.S.A.
Penguin Books Ltd, 27 Wrights Lane, London W8 5TZ, England
Penguin Books Australia Ltd, Ringwood, Victoria, Australia
Penguin Books Canada Ltd, 10 Alcorn Avenue, Toronto, Ontario, Canada M4V 3B2
Penguin Books (N.Z.) Ltd, 182–190 Wairau Road, Auckland 10, New Zealand

Penguin Books Ltd, Registered Offices: Harmondsworth, Middlesex, England

First published in Great Britain by Hamlyn Children's Books,
an imprint of Reed Children's Books, 1993
First published in the United States of America by Viking,
a division of Penguin Books USA Inc., 1994

1 3 5 7 9 10 8 6 4 2

Copyright © Reed International Books Ltd, 1993

All rights reserved.

Library of Congress Catalog Card Number: 94–60548

ISBN 0-670-85834-X

Printed in Belgium

CONTENTS

THE FAME OF THE VIKINGS

This bronze Scandinavian helmet was buried in a chieftain's grave in Sweden in the seventh century, before the Viking age.

Tales of the fierceness and brutality of the Vikings have endured through many centuries. Their skill as warriors, as boatbuilders, and as sailors is legendary. In this book we will find out, too, about their skills as fishers and farmers, the magnificence of their art, and their concern for the rule of law.

THE ORIGIN OF THE VIKINGS
The Vikings came from Scandinavia, from the countries we know today as Norway, Sweden, and Denmark. These countries were surrounded mostly by the sea, though their inland borders were not as well defined as those of modern countries. The Vikings all spoke the same language, Old Norse, and worshipped the same gods and goddesses.

The meaning of the name Viking is not certain. Its origin is possibly an Old Norse word *vik*, meaning bay or creek. In Norse, a *vikingr* was a pirate or raider. To the many people they conquered, the Vikings were known also as pagans, Danes, and Norsemen, or Northmen.

This figure of a buddha is evidence of the far-flung journeys and trading contacts of the Scandinavians even before the Viking age. Found in the port of Helgö in Sweden, it was made in northern India.

FJORDS AND FORESTS
The Vikings' homelands were extensive, stretching from northern Norway (inside the Arctic Circle) to the borders of Denmark, over 1,000 miles to the south. In Norway the land is very mountainous. Along the Norwegian coast the sea had penetrated the valleys, forming long, craggy inlets known as fjords. Many of Norway's inhabitants lived on small farms on the narrow coastal strip beside these fjords.

Sweden has many lakes and pine forests. Its people lived mainly in the central and southern parts of the country, where the best farmland was found. The sea around its coast was full of fish. In contrast, Denmark is a low-lying country that had some good agricultural land but much that was unsuitable for farming.

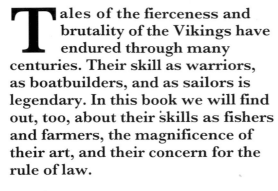

Western settlement
GREENLAND
Brattahlid
Thingvellir
Reykjavik
ICELAND

GREENLAND
"HELLULAND"
Brattahlid
"MARKLAND"
L'Anse aux Meadows
NEWFOUNDLAND
"VINLAND"

THE VIKING AGE
The "golden" period of the Scandinavian people, the Viking age, began at the end of the eighth century. The population was then about two million, but it had begun to grow quickly. The climate had improved and the harvests were good. The people used iron to make better tools and to improve their farming. Because they had more food, they lived longer and had more children.

At first the growing population was able to bring new land into cultivation. Gradually, though, good farming land became scarce, so many Vikings showed their spirit of adventure by seeking their fortune abroad.

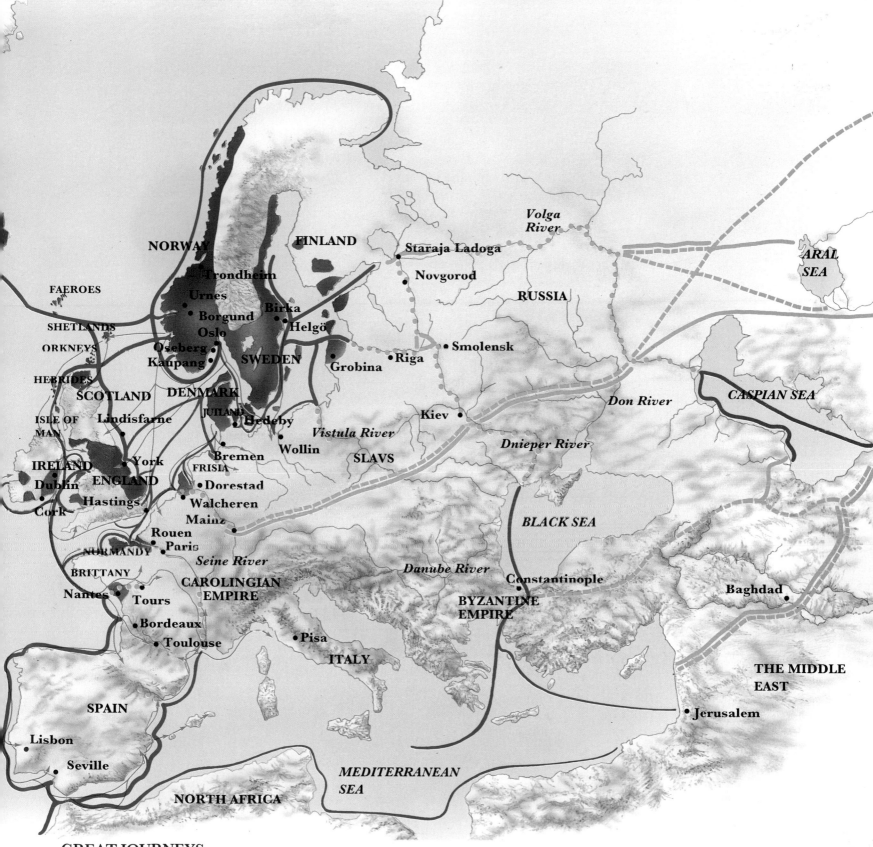

FAEROES

SHETLANDS

ORKNEYS

HEBRIDES

SCOTLAND

ISLE OF
MAN

IRELAND

Dublin

Cork

NORWAY

Trondheim

Urnes

Borgund

Oslo

Oseberg

Kaupang

DENMARK

JUTLAND

Hedeby

Lindisfarne

York

ENGLAND

Hastings

FINLAND

Birka

Helgö

SWEDEN

Grobina

Riga

Bremen

Wollin

Vistula River

SLAVS

FRISIA

Dorestad

Walcheren

Mainz

Rouen

Paris

Seine River

NORMANDY

BRITTANY

Nantes

Tours

Bordeaux

Toulouse

CAROLINGIAN
EMPIRE

Pisa

ITALY

SPAIN

Lisbon

Seville

MEDITERRANEAN
SEA

NORTH AFRICA

Staraja Ladoga

Novgorod

RUSSIA

Smolensk

Kiev

Volga
River

ARAL
SEA

Don River

CASPIAN SEA

Dnieper River

BLACK SEA

Danube River

Constantinople

BYZANTINE
EMPIRE

Baghdad

THE MIDDLE
EAST

Jerusalem

GREAT JOURNEYS

The Vikings built superb wooden ships
that enabled them to travel far and wide.
Their voyages opened up an exciting and
wealthy world. They journeyed farther
north and west than any Europeans had
gone before, went deep into Russia, and
opened trade routes to even more easterly
markets in Persia (Iran) and China.

This was a time of increasing trade and
prosperity in the Arab world and western
Europe, particularly in the Carolingian
Empire under Charlemagne. Soon the
enterprising Vikings had become a major
force in the economic and political life of
Europe. Their influence was unequaled
in Scandinavia's history.

Main areas of
settlement

Sea routes

River routes

Overland routes

Viking raids

International
trade routes

5

KINGS AND NOBLES

Viking society was clearly divided into classes. At the top of the social structure were the royal families. Viking kings were brave warriors who led their men in battle, and protected their people from pirates and invaders. They were usually the final authority in matters of law, and they acted as religious leaders.

ROYAL POWER

The kings came from ancient royal families, but wealth and royal blood were not always enough to keep them in power. A new king also had to be declared the rightful ruler by his free subjects — although the support of the chieftains and the reputation of his warriors could be very persuasive! A king who lost this support would be exiled or even killed. A cruel or unjust king could be legally overthrown.

The king's hall was the scene of many celebration banquets, where the king would reward his fighting men. Tables laden with food were arranged around a blazing log fire. The banqueters drank from drinking horns. These could not be put down until they were empty or else the beer or ale would spill out, so they were passed from person to person.

TRADE AND TAXATION

The kings were wealthy landowners and built up a network of royal estates. They needed plenty of silver to reward their supporters and to pay for the defense of their lands. Part of this wealth came as tribute from defeated enemies, such as Slav tribes in northeast Europe.

Some kings set up new market towns by the sea on good trade routes. Trade soon increased under royal protection from piracy, so the kings' representatives could collect even more tolls and taxes.

THE POWER OF THE CHIEFTAINS

Just below the kings were the chieftains, or nobles, who were landowners and warriors. These were the fierce Vikings who raided abroad and led the armies that terrorized much of western Europe in the ninth and tenth centuries. In early Viking times, many powerful chieftains had their own large war bands. They controlled vast areas of Scandinavia in almost complete independence.

As time passed the kings grew more successful in controlling the chieftains. They took away many of the chieftains' powers and gradually unified their lands under royal control.

THE RISE OF THE KINGDOMS

The separate nations of Norway, Sweden, and Denmark did not really exist until late in Viking times. However, there was a strong feeling of shared regional identity in spite of the frequent wars between the kings and chieftains. We know little about kings in Sweden, though Olof Skötkonung ruled over most of the country at the beginning of the eleventh century.

Denmark was the first to acquire a kind of unity, early in the ninth century. Its ruling family, or dynasty, produced a number of powerful kings. These included Harald Bluetooth (940–985), who drove the Swedes out of Denmark and for a time held sway over the king of Norway; and Canute "the Great" (ca.994–1035). Canute (also known as Cnut) was the most powerful Scandinavian king of the Viking age. By the end of his reign in 1035 he ruled over Denmark, part of Sweden, Norway, and England — a huge empire.

THE LAST GREAT VIKING

Norway was united in about 890 by Harald Finehair. Many Norwegian Vikings fled to escape his rule. Harald's great grandson was Olaf Tryggvason, a fierce king who converted Norway, Greenland, Iceland, and the Orkney and Faeroe Islands to Christianity.

Another Norwegian king, Harald Hardrada, was one of the last great figures of the Viking age. Harald traveled to Russia and the Byzantine Empire and married a Russian princess. He also campaigned in western Europe and attempted to restore Scandinavian power in England in the eleventh century. In 1066 Harald Hardrada was killed and his army defeated at the Battle of Stamford Bridge.

This illustration from an illuminated manuscript shows the martyrdom of St. Olaf, a famous Norwegian king.

Kings and nobles could afford many fine possessions, such as this magnificent carved chair.

7

As a sign of their authority in the home, Viking women carried big house keys fastened to their belts. These keys have sometimes been found buried in their graves.

The great majority of the Viking population was made up of freemen and slaves. All freemen had the right to appear before the public assembly, the *Thing*. They also had the right to carry arms. In contrast, the slaves had no rights. They formed the lowest class of Viking society.

FREEMEN

The wealth of individual freemen varied greatly. Some had large farms and owned as many as thirty slaves. Others were themselves employed by wealthy chieftains to work the chieftain's land.

Not all freemen were farmers. They could also be fishermen or boatbuilders, or even fine craftsmen, such as silversmiths. Many were skilled sailors and made up the crews of Viking longships.

A young boy and girl are sold into slavery by the Rus, their Viking captors. The Arab trader will pay with silver coins and other eastern luxuries. In Scandinavia, slaves were mainly bought to work on farms.

SLAVES

The slaves did all the hardest jobs around the house and on the land. Some of them were born in Scandinavia and may have been freemen who had lost their land and money. Many had been seized from their homes by raiding parties overseas.

Slaves had no rights at all. By law their master could beat them to death if he wished. Some of the luckier ones, such as skilled craftsmen, seem to have been treated quite well. They were even paid for the work they did and were able to save up and buy their freedom.

THE SLAVE TRADE

The slave trade was an important source of wealth to the Vikings. Slave traders were said to be the richest of all the Viking merchants. They captured large numbers of healthy-looking people who were then sold for silver and gold. When they looted monasteries, the Vikings often seized high-ranking churchmen to exchange for a ransom from the Church or their families.

VIKING WOMEN

It is difficult to draw general conclusions about the lives of Viking women. They varied greatly in different parts of Scandinavia and at different periods. It does seem that Scandinavian women were greatly respected. A man who courted a Viking girl by kissing her, or by writing her a love song, was expected to marry her. If he did not, he might suffer blood vengeance from her father and brothers. If a married couple divorced, the husband usually had to pay back any dowry to the wife's family.

As in other early societies, many women were concerned mainly with taking care of children, looking after the home, and making and washing clothes. Other women owned property, and they seem to have been very independent. Women often ran the family farms for months on end because their husbands were away fighting or trading. However, women had no political rights, such as attending formal sessions of the Thing.

Women had the task of running the farm while their husbands were away. This woman is looking after her children, feeding the chickens, and at the same time, supervising a clumsy farmhand!

FAITHFUL TO THE END

Viking sagas tell us of very faithful wives who stand by their husbands to the end. One of them, Bergthora, refuses to leave her husband's side to escape from their blazing farmhouse, saying:

I was given young to Njal, and I have promised him that one fate shall fall on us both.

— *Njal's Saga* —

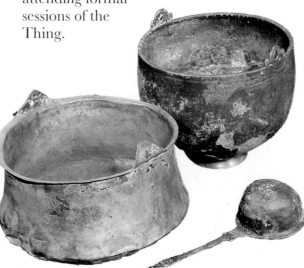

Archaeologists have found many objects placed in women's graves, such as iron and copper caldrons (shown here), bowls, caskets, combs, brooches, beads, and pendants, as well as wine jugs and drinking glasses. Many of these objects are as valuable as those found in men's graves.

FARMING AND FOOD

Beautifully decorated silver drinking cups were given to warriors who had performed valiantly in battle.

The Vikings had to work hard to make a living from farming their homelands. In northern Scandinavia, part of which is inside the Arctic Circle, the climate was very cold. In winter the rivers could freeze for months at a time, and the summers were often too brief for crops to ripen properly. Farther south the climate was more kind, and Viking farmers could grow a range of crops such as barley, wheat, rye, peas, and beans.

THE FARMSTEAD

Families lived in low wooden or stone longhouses. The roof was usually made of reeds or straw, although sometimes turf was used. The walls of some buildings were supported with wooden posts, to help hold the weight of the roof.

Next to the house were other, smaller, buildings, such as a cowshed, barns, a smithy, a bathhouse, and a smokehouse for preserving meat and fish.

A wealthy Viking freeman might have many slaves to help him farm the land and do the chores. On smaller farms the whole family would have to work in the fields and look after the animals.

He tamed the oxen and tempered plowshares, timbered houses and barns for the hay, fashioned carts, and followed the plow.

— Viking poem —

A HARD LIFE

On good land, several farms would be grouped together in a settlement. Where the land was poor, only one or two families could work the land. Small fields were scratched out on the hillsides with a small plow called an *ard*. This was a crooked, pointed piece of wood that could be pulled behind an ox and guided by one person. Some ards were tipped with iron to make them sharper. Plows that could turn the soil over properly were not used in Scandinavia until the eleventh century.

This longhouse and its other buildings have turf roofs that will keep them dry and warm in winter. The farm occupies an excellent site close to the sea for fishing and possibly trade. Women are washing clothes in the stream.

10

A SIMPLE DIET

In winter, food was often scarce. For most people the staple diet was porridge and bread made from barley and oats; the climate was not warm enough to grow much wheat. Sheep, cattle, pigs, and goats provided meat and dairy products as well as clothing. Because it was difficult to feed animals during the winter months, all but the strongest beasts were killed at the end of the autumn. Their meat was smoked or salted for eating during the winter.

FEASTING

The Vikings liked to hold great feasts, especially in celebration of trading and military expeditions. A successful feast would earn great honor for the host. The banqueters sat at tables facing into the middle of the hall. Meat — beef, pork, and lamb — would be stewed or roasted on a spit in the kitchen area, and then carried into the hall.

The food was seasoned with garlic and mustard or, in very rich households, spices from the East. There was no sugar, but honey was used as a sweetener and in making a drink called mead. The Vikings also ate plenty of small loaves of bread baked in round pans.

SOMETHING TO DRINK

Beer was brewed from barley. On special occasions, wine imported from France and Germany was drunk by the rich. Vikings probably got very drunk at feasts, sometimes to celebrate — or forget — the bloody battles they had fought.

The Vikings were proud of their hospitality and fine meals. This woman is preparing bread, apples, and fish, while more food simmers on the hearth.

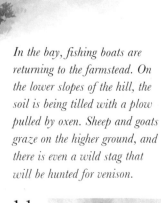

In the bay, fishing boats are returning to the farmstead. On the lower slopes of the hill, the soil is being tilled with a plow pulled by oxen. Sheep and goats graze on the higher ground, and there is even a wild stag that will be hunted for venison.

11

HUNTING AND FISHING

These fishhooks come from the English city of York, where fish played an important part in the diet of the Viking townspeople.

In many parts of Scandinavia the land was unsuitable for farming, so hunting for food was essential. Fortunately the great forests were the homes of many animals — elk, deer, wild boar, and bears — and the seas were full of fish.

WILD GAME

In the north the larger animals were hunted with spears and bows and arrows, occasionally from horseback. Although animals were hunted mainly for meat, little was wasted. Bone and antler were used for making knife handles and combs, and the skins and furs were turned into warm clothes.

Hunting wild animals on horseback became a popular pastime among some wealthy Vikings who could afford fast horses. These hunters will need great skill to spear their quarry as they gallop by.

In those mountains there are such large numbers of big game that the greatest part of the country subsists only on the beasts of the forest. Buffaloes, aurochs [wild oxen], and elk are taken there.

— *Adam of Bremen* —

Smaller creatures, too, were hunted and trapped. Hares and ducks were commonly eaten at Viking feasts, as were the eggs of seabirds. Collecting eggs from the nests high on the cliffs required a strong head for heights!

FISH

Nets, hooks, floats, and weights have been found in many Viking settlements, showing the importance of fishing to the local people. People in Hedeby, York, and Birka seem to have eaten a lot of fish, because the bones of cod, haddock, herring, and eels have been found in these big towns. In parts of Denmark, where crops were more plentiful, people might have fished partly for sport.

GREENLAND

Hunting and fishing were very important in Greenland. This land was explored by a Norwegian Viking called Eric the Red, who had been banished from Iceland for committing a murder. In about A.D. 986 he encouraged others to settle there. The first intrepid settlers set out from Iceland in twenty-five ships, but some were lost and others turned back. The survivors founded the settlement of Brattahlid, where they later built a small church.

They found that Greenland was not very green, despite its name. Although there was fertile land on the south and west coasts, where they had landed, much of the island was covered with glaciers and snow. The settlers had to make use of all Greenland's natural resources to survive. They raised animals, hunted and fished, and traded with merchants in Iceland and Scandinavia.

BOUNTY FROM THE SEA

The settlers found there were plenty of fish, seals, walruses, and whales around the coast. Fish was eaten fresh, or dried and salted for when the sea was too rough for fishing trips. A saga also tells that the Vikings chased whales from the open sea into the coastal bays. There they drove the whales onto the beaches and killed them with spears or perhaps harpoons. As well as hunting seals and walruses, they even captured and killed the polar bears that roamed the glaciers — which must have been very dangerous.

The Greenlanders made warm fur coats from sealskins, and carved the ivory walrus tusks into caskets and ornaments. They made the bones of whales into food containers. These precious goods were then exchanged for wheat, iron, and timber from Iceland and Europe.

The Vikings ate seabirds and their eggs. Collecting eggs from nests high up on sheer cliff faces was often dangerous, especially while seabirds wheeled and screeched around the nests.

In the icy wastes of the north, hunters could make a fortune from sealskins — but the cold was not the only danger.

13

ONE OF THE FAMILY

Viking children were the pride of their parents. Because life was so hard, many children probably died before they reached adulthood. Those who did survive must have been very strong and independent.

These miniature figures found in the Outer Hebrides in Scotland were used in board games. They were made of walrus ivory late in the Viking age.

DEATH OR SURVIVAL

Although there was an ancient law that allowed babies to be killed, this happened very rarely. Only those babies that looked like they could not survive the rigors of Viking life, or babies born when there was a famine, were left outside to die.

Most new babies were welcomed into the family. They were given a name, sprinkled with water, and then lifted onto their father's knee as a sign of acceptance into the family. They were given presents to mark the occasion, and later received another one when they cut their first tooth.

A BUSY CHILDHOOD

As soon as children were old enough, their parents began to teach them all they knew. Girls were taught how to spin and weave by their mothers, and boys went out in fishing boats with their fathers. Both worked on the family farm. They took the pigs to market, scared birds away from the crops, and helped at home with baking, weaving, smoking fish, making butter, and many other household tasks. Children were also taught the runes (see page 42).

Although they worked hard, children also found time to play. In the cold northern winters they skated on icy ponds, wearing shoes with bone skates attached. We know they had balls and other wooden and fabric toys, although few of these have survived.

Boys' games trained them to be good soldiers when they grew up. According to a Viking poet, the sons of freemen and nobles learned "to shoot arrows, ride on horseback, hunt with hounds, brandish swords, and do feats of swimming." Only the oldest son would inherit the family land, so younger sons often used their military skills in raiding or as mercenaries.

GAMES

Children and their parents enjoyed board games, which they played during the long winter evenings in the light cast by a blazing fire or oil lamps. Using pieces made of bone or glass, they played a kind of checkers on wooden boards. Another favorite game was *hnefatafl*. The board and counters of this game were something like those used for chess, but the rules were different. These games were probably invented by the Vikings. Travelers brought some other games from the East.

MARRIAGE

Marriage between young people was probably arranged between heads of families, but Viking poetry often describes the beauty of falling in love or the sadness of losing a lover.

In one of the Viking sagas the god Frey persuades Gerd to become his bride, but she says he will have to wait for her for nine nights. Frey says:

Long is a night, longer are two.
How shall I throle [bear] three?
Shorter to me a month oft seemed,
than half this hovering time.

Viking saga

FAMILIES

Members of Viking families — including aunts, uncles, and cousins — were very loyal to one another. They would all support their family in a disagreement with another family. The worst arguments, started when a person was killed by a member of a different family, were called blood feuds. Feuds would lead to revenge killings — blood vengeance — and bloody fights, and often lasted for years.

A brother and sister play a board game as their father carves wood. Their mother is looking after a caldron of soup suspended above the fire.

A badly wounded man is tended by his friend as his attacker is held back by two companions. The attack might lead to a blood feud.

The first coins minted in Denmark came from Hedeby. Very similar to silver coins minted by the Carolingian Empire, most had ship designs, though some show animals or buildings.

Many Vikings lived in small village communities or on isolated farmsteads. As international trade developed, some big market towns grew up. Hedeby, in Viking-age Denmark, was one such trading center.

FOUNDATION OF HEDEBY

Hedeby was established by King Godfred of Denmark, who had dared to challenge the powerful Carolingian Emperor Charlemagne. Although Godfred failed to defeat Charlemagne, he destroyed a trading center called Reric and moved its merchants to Hedeby in about A.D. 808. This new town was at the base of the Jutland peninsula, where the trade routes linking the North Sea, the Baltic Sea, and western Europe came together.

Hedeby eventually became waterlogged. This preserved many wooden structures and wooden and leather objects. Hedeby's orderly layout, ditches, and earthworks suggest it was a prosperous and well-governed town. This scene shows part of the town, with ships on the shore, and one of the gateways in the earthwork.

Because of its good position, Hedeby quickly became the largest Scandinavian town of the age. Its population of about ten thousand seems to have depended on craftwork and trade, rather than on farming, for their livelihood.

A stream flowed through the town center from east to west, channeled to control its flow. Inside the town, straight roads made of wooden planks were laid parallel and at right angles to the stream.

DEFENSES

The town had a semicircular rampart and was also linked to the *Danevirke*, defenses developed by Godfred to protect the southern borders of his kingdom. At first Hedeby was protected by a simple wooden stockade. Later, in the tenth century, a huge earthwork was made. It had three gateways in it, to the north, south, and west, and was roughly 30 feet high. Parts of the earthwork are visible today.

In 1066, the same year the battles of Stamford Bridge and Hastings took place in England, Hedeby was attacked by an army of Slavs. It never recovered, and nearby Schleswig took over most of its trade.

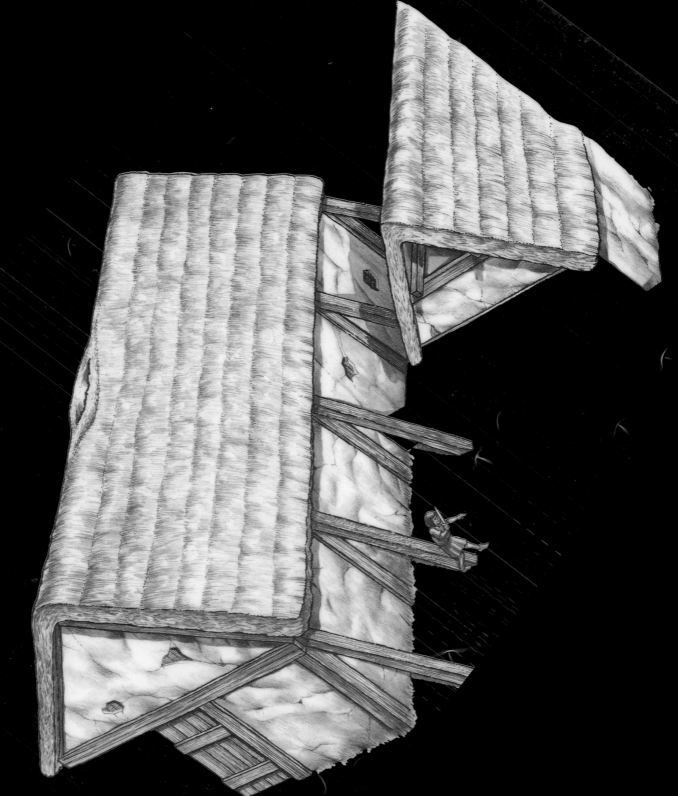

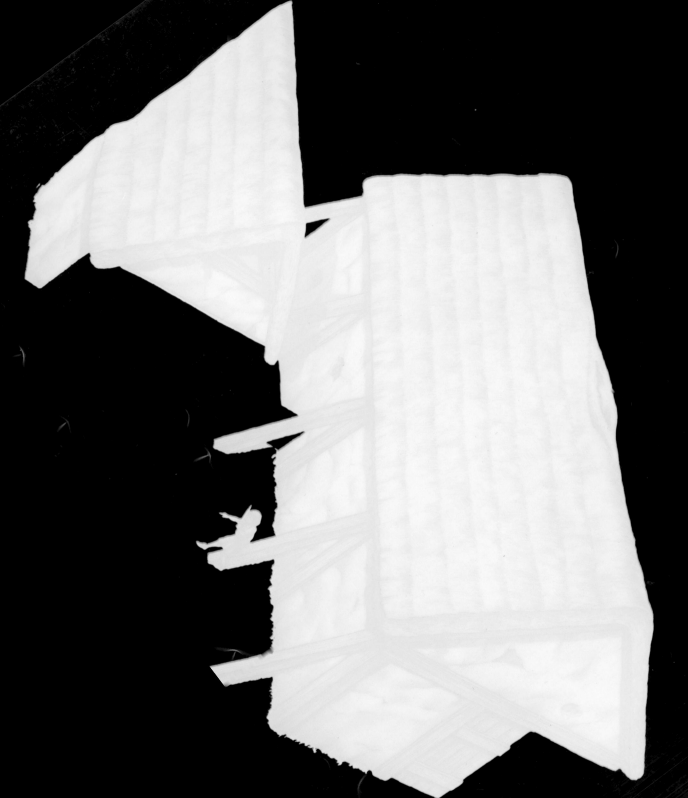

TOWN HOUSES

Room for all the family

Most of Hedeby's houses, which were laid out with one end facing the street, had timber frames and walls made of wattle and daub (wickerwork coated with mud or clay). Others had a stave construction. Their walls were made of tree trunks cut lengthways and placed side by side in the ground. The average size of a town house was 20 feet by 50 feet. One quite elaborate house had three internal rooms and a bread oven, as well as a hearth. Almost every house had its own workshop, yard, and trash pit, and some had their own timber-lined wells. There were also small buildings with floors dug down below the surrounding ground level. These might have been used as workshops.

1 Wattle and daub walls
2 Timber frame
3 Workshop
4 Bread oven
5 Hearth
6 Seating and sleeping platform
7 Packed earth floor
8 Storage chest
9 Storehouse

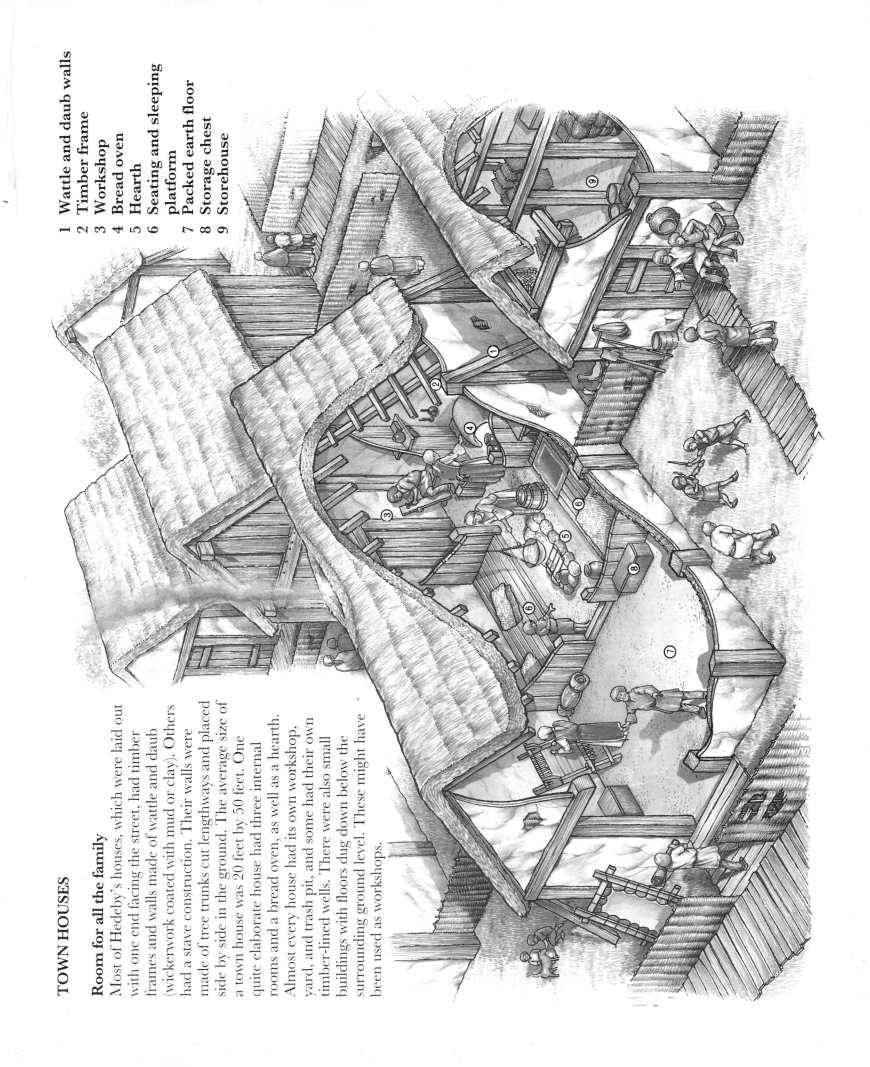

CLOTHES AND WEAVING

Carved whalebone plaques have been found in the graves of rich Viking women in Norway. They may have been used for smoothing or pleating cloth by winding the wet cloth around them and leaving it to dry.

Despite the difficult and often unsanitary conditions in which they lived, many Vikings took great care of their appearance. Most clothes were produced at home. The wealthy also imitated and imported fashions from western Europe.

MAKING CLOTHES

Women, who were expected to be skilled at spinning and weaving, usually made the family's clothes. The wool came from the family's sheep, which were sheared late in spring. It had to be cleaned of dirt and grease before it could be combed using special iron-toothed combs called cards.

The wool was then spun on a spindle weighted with a "whorl" of clay, stone, or bone. Being very fond of bright colors, the Vikings dyed the wool in many shades, including red, green, yellow, purple, orange, and blue. The women then wove the wool into cloth on an upright loom.

THE LOOM

The loom had two upright wooden posts that leaned against the wall in the main room of the house. These posts supported a horizontal beam from which hung the warp (the vertical threads, which were weighted with clay or stone fastened at the bottom). The weaver passed the weft (the horizontal threads) through the warp, gradually producing the woven cloth.

Sometimes delicate pieces of imported silk were sewn onto the finished garments. On special occasions fine linen was worn, as were patterned silks and embroideries imported by the rich.

Spinning and weaving took up much of women's time. The woman in the middle is carefully carding the wool to disentangle the fibers. On the right the wool is being spun into long threads on a spindle. On the left the weaver is sitting at her loom. She is pushing the horizontal thread — the weft — in and out of the warp, to produce the finished cloth.

WOMEN'S FASHIONS

A tenth-century poem describes a Viking woman as wearing a smock with brooches on the shoulders, a neckerchief, and a headdress. The smock was a long linen or woolen tunic with a type of pleated pinafore dress over the top. The brooches were not only for show, but fastened the shoulder straps of the dress. When a Viking woman went out she might also wear a thick shawl or cloak to keep her warm and dry.

Single girls could wear their hair loose, with a band, but married women always kept their heads covered with scarves or a headdress. They also wore their hair long, but pulled into a soft bun at the back of the head.

FRAGMENTARY EVIDENCE

Tiny fragments of Viking clothes have sometimes been found in graves. Usually the material has completely rotted away over the centuries, but, just occasionally, little pieces close to metal brooches or weapons have been preserved. When the Vikings became Christians they stopped burying their dead fully dressed and wearing brooches, and so this form of evidence disappeared.

MEN'S CLOTHES

A frayed tapestry found in the Oseberg ship burial (see page 33) shows Viking men wearing tightly fitting tunics and baggy trousers. Others wear bright cloaks with pointed ends. We also know that men wore pants that were quite narrowly cut and looked more like leggings. Trousers were held up by sashes or leather belts with buckles.

Over the top were worn furs, hides, and heavy woolen cloaks. If the owner was rich, these might have gold braid woven into them. The cloak was fixed by a brooch on one shoulder so that the other arm could move freely, perhaps to reach for a sharp knife worn on the belt.

Vikings were proud of their appearance and probably washed frequently. In Iceland there is evidence they bathed in the hot springs, as these young men are doing. Some Viking homes might have had a saunalike bathhouse.

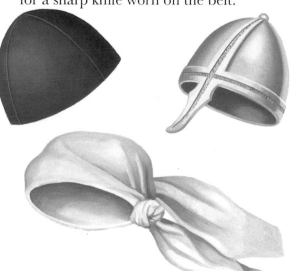

The Vikings wore all sorts of hats, scarves, and headdresses to keep their heads warm, as well as leather caps and helmets for protection. Viking warriors never wore helmets with horns on them!

This fabulous crystal pendant was found in Sweden near the site of a Viking harbor. A Viking craftsman probably mounted the imported crystal in the silver.

The Vikings were no different from other peoples — if they had wealth and status, they displayed it by wearing fine clothes and beautiful jewelry. Some jewelry, such as cloak brooches, had a practical purpose, while other items were worn purely for decoration.

A SIGN OF WEALTH

In the tenth century, Ibn Fadlan, an Arab traveling along the Volga River in Russia, described how Viking women carried containers made of iron, silver, copper, or gold around their necks. The size and substance of the container depended on the husband's wealth. Attached to the container was a ring carrying a knife.

Round her neck she wears gold or silver rings. When a man amasses 10,000 dirhams [Arabic silver coins] he makes his wife one gold ring, when he has 20,000 he makes two; and so a woman gets a new ring for every 10,000 dirhams her husband acquires.

— Ibn Fadlan —

He then described how women might have many of these neck rings. We know also that both men and women wore arm rings, as well as finger rings.

FINE CRAFTSMANSHIP

Judging by the high standard of workmanship, making jewelry must have been a specialized craft. Most jewelry would have come from specialist craftsmen in the towns.

The most practical form of jewelry was the brooch. The rich could afford brooches made of silver and gold. Poorer people had to make do with cheaper ones of bronze or lead alloy that looked like silver. These were often gilded or tinned in imitation of the more expensive versions. The gold and silver had to be imported from the East, exacted as tribute, or seized in raids. However, some copper was mined in Scandinavia.

CASTING

Bronze brooches were cast in clay molds. The craftsman fired the clay mold (baked it hard) so that it would not shatter during the casting. He also had to heat the bronze to over 1,200°F so that it could be poured into the fired mold. For elaborate pieces, the design was first modeled in wax, as shown below. Craftsmen could also mass-produce simpler designs by pressing an object into clay to make a series of molds.

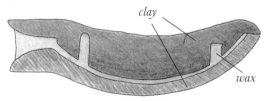

clay

wax

Jewelry made from jet was much prized by wealthy Viking women. Here the jet has been carved in the form of two beasts gripping each other, a favorite Scandinavian design.

Three stages in casting a bronze brooch. The mold was modeled from clay, using wax to form the shape of the brooch. The wax was melted and poured out, then molten bronze was poured into the mold. When the bronze had cooled, the clay mold was broken to release the brooch.

NECKLACES

Necklaces of beads were often strung between the brooches. The beads were made of carnelian, crystals, amber, silver, or colored glass. Personal objects such as needles and combs could be hung from the brooches on a chain.

Bead-making was another skilled craft. Rough glass was imported from western Europe in the form of cubes and lumps. These were melted and pulled into sticks that were wound around metal rods. Trails of glass in other colors were mixed in to produce brilliant multicolored beads.

BROOCH DESIGN

In the ninth and tenth centuries the dress brooches worn by women were oval (tortoiseshell) shaped. They were about 4 or 5 inches long and covered with stylized animal patterns. In the late Viking period they became less well made and less fashionable. Women started to wear shawls over them, in some regions pinned by smaller "equal-armed" (three-pointed) brooches.

A Viking woman carefully pins her oval brooch to her woolen tunic.

Silver earrings (left), a fashion copied from the Slavs, have sometimes been found in rich Viking graves in Sweden.

Amber (above) is a fossilized resin that washes up on beaches. It was used for jewelry from very early times. Supplies of amber were sent to towns like York and Hedeby to be worked into beads.

Shown at the far left are two bronze oval or "tortoiseshell" brooches, and a "trefoil" or equal-armed brooch. The brooches on the left, with the beads of carnelian, rock crystal, and glass, were found in a wealthy woman's grave at Birka, in Sweden.

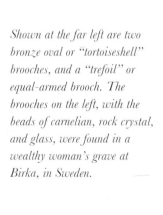

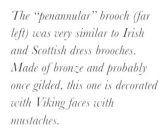

The "penannular" brooch (far left) was very similar to Irish and Scottish dress brooches. Made of bronze and probably once gilded, this one is decorated with Viking faces with mustaches.

The Borre style is shown on this silver brooch.

This horse harness has decoration in the Jellinge style.

The Mammen style is named after an ax found in Mammen, Jutland. It has a design of a winged lion entangled in foliage, inlaid with silver wire.

The Ringerike style can be seen carved on a tombstone found in the churchyard of St. Paul's Cathedral in London.

The Vikings were skilled at many forms of arts and crafts. They excelled in decorating ordinary objects such as combs, buckets, and sleds. In the towns there were craft quarters, where people could buy goods made of metal, leather, or wood. These were possibly made in small workshops behind the craftsmen's houses.

ART

For centuries Scandinavian art had consisted mainly of patterns of interlinked animals twisting round or gripping each other. This interest in animal styles continued throughout the Viking period, changing slowly as it was influenced by art from outside Scandinavia.

ART STYLES

There were several styles of Viking art. The earliest was the Borre style, named after a rich burial in Norway. It features animal heads and interlaced braids, and sometimes has a "gripping beast," a ribbonlike animal with paws that grip its own body. The Jellinge style was next. Its animals have a ribbonlike body and a sort of pigtail. The Mammen style grew out of the Jellinge style, introducing animals with more substantial bodies, and makes much use of plant patterns called tendrils.

After the Mammen style came the Ringerike style. The animal's limbs seem to turn into the long leaves of the acanthus plant and the long, curly tendrils often dominate the whole pattern. The last style is the Urnes style, named after carving on a small Norwegian church built in about 1060 at a place called Urnes. The animals, interlaced and biting each other, are thin and graceful with delicate heads and pointed eyes.

METALWORK

Metalwork was one of the Vikings' greatest skills, and the smith had an important place in Viking society. Iron ore, easily found in the bogs of Scandinavia, was smelted in furnaces fueled by charcoal.

Excavations of smithies have revealed that their craftsmen used most of the tools known to nineteenth-century blacksmiths. Large farms had their own forges. Smaller farms probably used the services of a traveling smith, who carried his tools with him.

This beautiful gold cross from Ireland, the Cross of Cong, is decorated in the Urnes style.

WOOD CARVING

Wood was abundant in Scandinavian forests, and it is certain that wood carving was practiced widely. Burial graves contain many beautifully carved goods, such as wagons, and houses were decorated with carvings. Sadly, though, wood does not survive very often, and so the greater part of Viking art may be lost to us.

Skill in woodworking was not limited to decorating objects, however. As we shall see on the next pages, the Vikings were master boatbuilders.

Smithies were probably much like those of later medieval times. There was a charcoal fire for heating the metals, and a pair of bellows that was used by the smith's assistant to keep the fire burning. The smith would grasp the red-hot iron with his tongs and hammer it into shape on an anvil.

PATTERN WELDING

A process called pattern welding was used by the Viking smith to make swords strong and flexible. He welded together iron bars, twisting them around each other to form light and dark patterns along the blade. This pattern would show up beautifully when the weapon was polished. The sword was usually completed by adding a sharp cutting edge of better-quality iron.

23

VIKING SHIPS

This reconstructed anchor, made from wood and weighed down by a large rock, was found in Norway. It is almost ten feet long.

This is a high-sided merchant ship. It has a large cargo hold in the middle of the deck, but only a few oars.

The Vikings' ships were the high technology of their time. They allowed the Vikings to dominate much of Europe for more than two hundred years as they traveled hundreds of miles, trading and raiding.

THE EARLY SHIPS

Early Scandinavian ships had no keel, so journeys in bad weather and strong currents were difficult. By the Viking age, Scandinavian shipbuilders had introduced the oak keel, which gave their boats much greater stability. They also added a mast and sail, and now the Vikings could make much longer journeys.

Viking ships were very strong, but light. The keel (the ship's backbone) was usually made of a single piece of oak. Attached to this were the stem (front) and the stern (back). The hull was then made from overlapping side planks, or strakes, which were nailed together. The ship had a deck and was waterproofed with pitch.

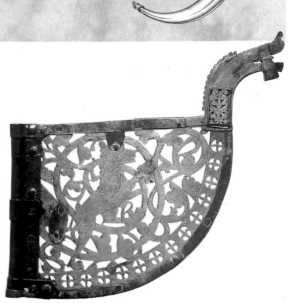

This weather vane, made of gilt bronze, was once fixed to the prow of a Viking ship. It is beautifully engraved with a great beast in the Ringerike style. Perhaps the beast is meant to be gazing at the distant horizon.

TRADE AND WAR

At first the same sort of ship was used for both trade and warfare. By the tenth century, however, ships were being built for special purposes. Short, broad merchant vessels could carry up to 35 tons of cargo, including horses and cattle. The longer, slimmer warships, or longships, had a combination of many oars and a sail. This gave them great maneuverability and speed, even in difficult conditions.

THE LONGSHIPS

Most longships had about sixteen or eighteen benches, or rowing seats, on each side, seating a minimum of thirty-two or thirty-six rowers. The oarsmen sat either on benches or perhaps on chests that contained their personal possessions. They had to row with all their strength and bail out sea water in bad weather. The life of a rower certainly was not easy.

One giant longship, belonging to King Olaf Tryggvasson in about 998, had thirty-four benches on each side and was known as the *Long Serpent*. Its prow, or stem, was carved with the proud head of a dragon. No wonder the sight of longships terrified the people of Europe!

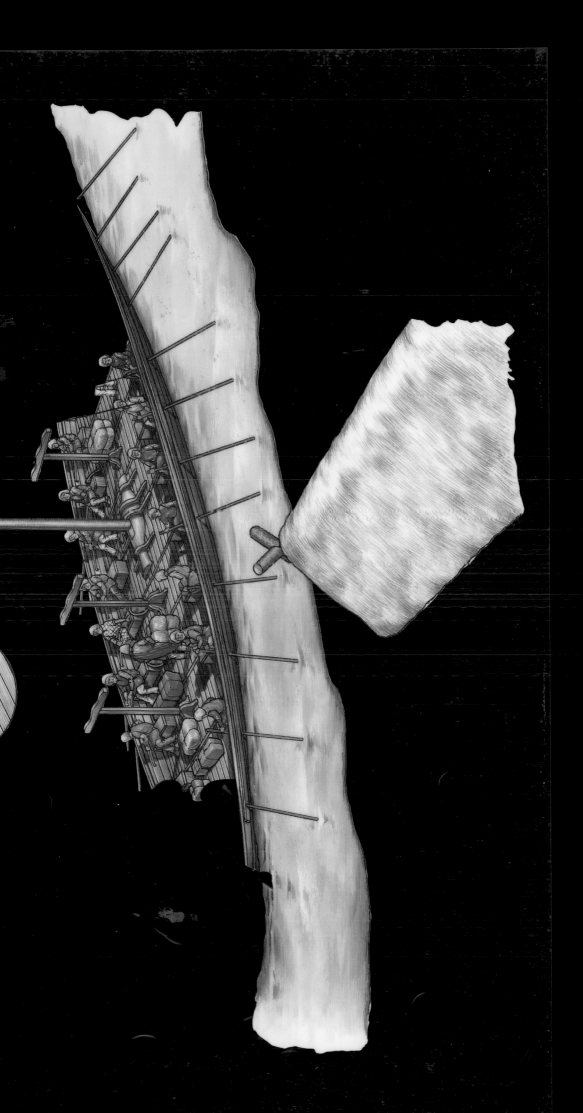

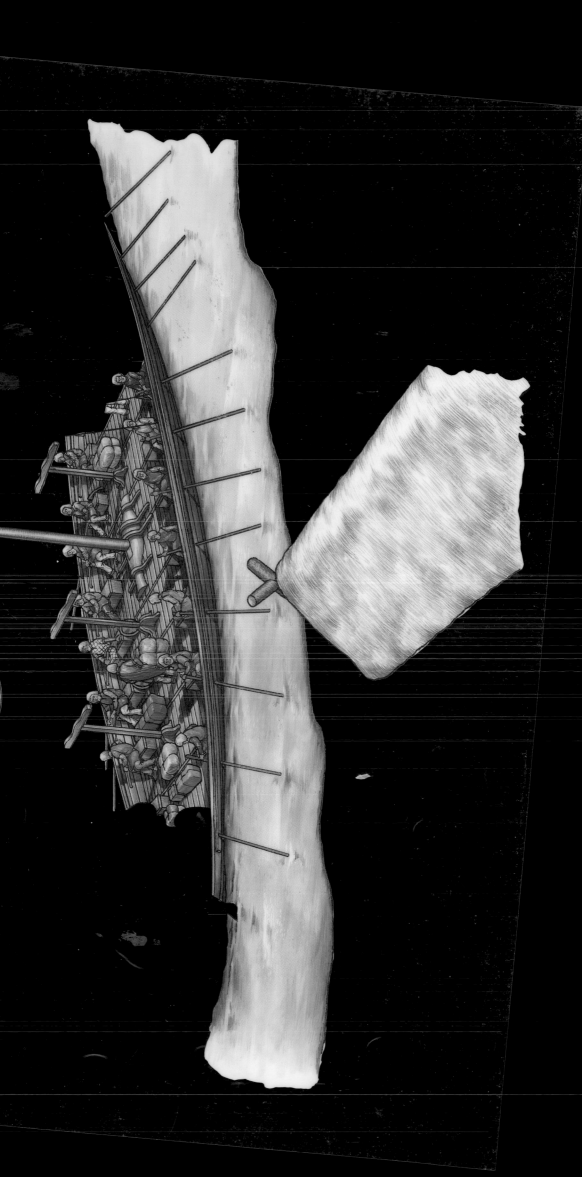

WOOD CARVING

Wood was abundant in Scandinavian forests, and it is certain that wood carving was practiced widely. Burial graves contain many beautifully carved goods, such as wagons, and houses were decorated with carvings. Sadly, though, wood does not survive very often, and so the greater part of Viking art may be lost to us.

Skill in woodworking was not limited to decorating objects, however. As we shall see on the next pages, the Vikings were master boatbuilders.

Smithies were probably much like those of later medieval times. There was a charcoal fire for heating the metals, and a pair of bellows that was used by the smith's assistant to keep the fire burning. The smith would grasp the red-hot iron with his tongs and hammer it into shape on an anvil.

PATTERN WELDING

A process called pattern welding was used by the Viking smith to make swords strong and flexible. He welded together iron bars, twisting them around each other to form light and dark patterns along the blade. This pattern would show up beautifully when the weapon was polished. The sword was usually completed by adding a sharp cutting edge of better-quality iron.

VIKING SHIPS

The Vikings' ships were the high technology of their time. They allowed the Vikings to dominate much of Europe for more than two hundred years as they traveled hundreds of miles, trading and raiding.

This reconstructed anchor, made from wood and weighed down by a large rock, was found in Norway. It is almost ten feet long.

This is a high-sided merchant ship. It has a large cargo hold in the middle of the deck, but only a few oars.

THE EARLY SHIPS

Early Scandinavian ships had no keel, so journeys in bad weather and strong currents were difficult. By the Viking age, Scandinavian shipbuilders had introduced the oak keel, which gave their boats much greater stability. They also added a mast and sail, and now the Vikings could make much longer journeys.

Viking ships were very strong, but light. The keel (the ship's backbone) was usually made of a single piece of oak. Attached to this were the stem (front) and the stern (back). The hull was then made from overlapping side planks, or strakes, which were nailed together. The ship had a deck and was waterproofed with pitch.

This weather vane, made of gilt bronze, was once fixed to the prow of a Viking ship. It is beautifully engraved with a great beast in the Ringerike style. Perhaps the beast is meant to be gazing at the distant horizon.

TRADE AND WAR

At first the same sort of ship was used for both trade and warfare. By the tenth century, however, ships were being built for special purposes. Short, broad merchant vessels could carry up to 35 tons of cargo, including horses and cattle. The longer, slimmer warships, or longships, had a combination of many oars and a sail. This gave them great maneuverability and speed, even in difficult conditions.

THE LONGSHIPS

Most longships had about sixteen or eighteen benches, or rowing seats, on each side, seating a minimum of thirty-two or thirty-six rowers. The oarsmen sat either on benches or perhaps on chests that contained their personal possessions. They had to row with all their strength and bail out sea water in bad weather. The life of a rower certainly was not easy.

One giant longship, belonging to King Olaf Tryggvasson in about 998, had thirty-four benches on each side and was known as the *Long Serpent*. Its prow, or stem, was carved with the proud head of a dragon. No wonder the sight of longships terrified the people of Europe!

A VIKING LONGSHIP

Dragon ship

The Vikings' fast and maneuverable longships could sail at over 7 knots (miles per hour) in good conditions. If the wind dropped, they lowered the sail and rowed instead. A raiding party could sail from Denmark to England in under two days. The ships also had a shallow draft (depth beneath the water) and were very light and flexible. This meant they could be rowed up rivers and dragged onto beaches. In the winter, ships and boats were stored in boat sheds called *nausts*.

Mast support

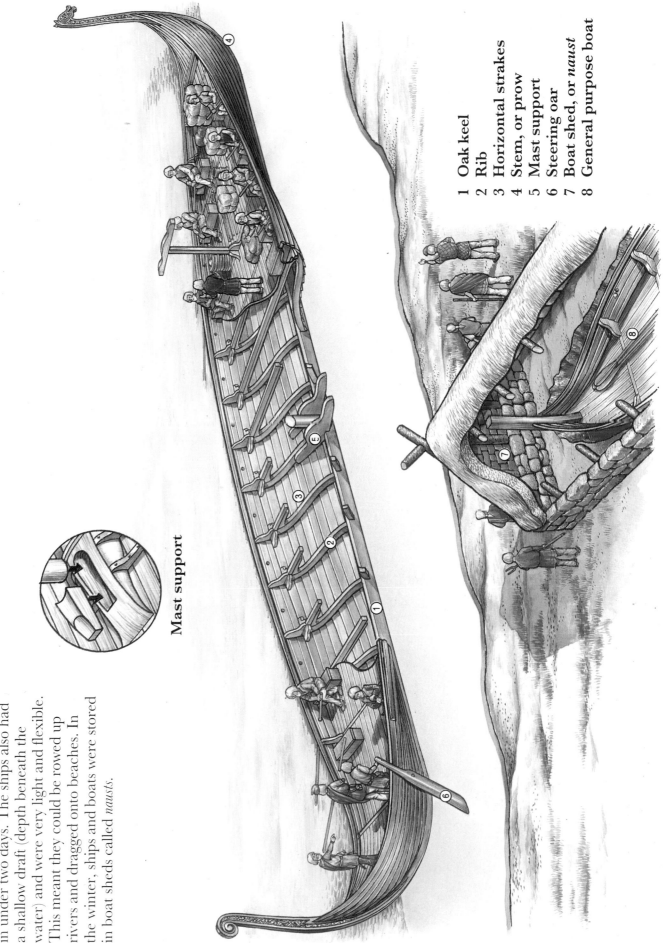

1 Oak keel
2 Rib
3 Horizontal strakes
4 Stem, or prow
5 Mast support
6 Steering oar
7 Boat shed, or *naust*
8 General purpose boat

The Vikings did not use coins very much. Instead, merchants relied on silver. They weighed it out carefully on small pairs of scales that they always carried with them.

Although they could row great distances along rivers, Viking adventurers sometimes had to haul their ships overland.

Viking merchants traveled huge distances to trade. They set off with goods such as walrus ivory, skins, furs, hunting falcons, amber, and slaves, and returned with silks, spices, and silver from the East. They also brought back luxuries such as exotic jewelry, French and German wines, and glassware and fine pottery from the Rhineland.

ALL SORTS OF TRADERS

Some traders were full-time merchants, or craftsmen selling their products. Others sold booty from raids, or goods they had received as tribute. Many Vikings who were normally farmers went on summer trading expeditions. Perhaps this was to supplement their income in harsh times, or just for the adventure.

FELLOWSHIPS

Some Vikings joined together in fellowships, to share the costs, risks, and benefits of an enterprise. Called a *felag*, a fellowship was often a trading partnership, but it might also be a band of mercenaries or a craftsmen's guild, for example.

TRAVELS IN THE EAST

The Vikings headed across the Baltic Sea, setting up trading stations beside the main rivers. Many traders pressed on to sell their furs and slaves in Russia. It must have been an arduous journey. These intrepid Vikings were called the *Rus*, or foreigners, hence the name Russia. They founded the cities of Novgorod, Kiev, and Smolensk, and opened up Russia to trade. The Rus proved so adaptable to local conditions and politics that they ruled these areas as princes until the eleventh century.

Even this did not satisfy some Vikings. They went on to the Black Sea and to the Byzantine capital of Constantinople, over 1,000 miles from Scandinavia! There were so many Vikings in Constantinople (which they called Miklagard) that part of the city became known as the Vikings' quarter.

> He gathered a company of sixty men and five women. He made an agreement with his crew that everyone should share equally in whatever profits the expedition might yield.
>
> —*The Greenland Saga*

MARKET CENTERS

At the beginning of the ninth century a number of market towns began to grow up alongside the main trade routes. A very early one was Helgö on an island in Lake Mälar in Sweden. Craft workshops and goods from the East and West have been found there. Helgö later declined in importance and the nearby town of Birka replaced it. Birka soon dominated trade with the East.

Traders traveled across the lake to Birka, mooring their boats in the harbor. In the winter when the lake froze over, they went on skis and by sleds.

TRADE IN THE WEST

In the West there were already many trading routes, some along the roads of the old Roman Empire, or the routes set up by the Carolingians. As we have seen on page 16, Hedeby in Jutland was the most important center of trade in Scandinavia. Dublin and York, too, became prosperous in the late ninth century. Between the two towns there was much coming and going across England and the Irish Sea.

Even in harsh winter weather, Vikings traveled to trading centers such as Birka. They probably carried their goods on sleds, and skied over the snow. They also skated on the frozen lakes, though they kept their skates on the ice and used poles to push themselves forward.

Arabic silver coins (above), called dirhams, were brought to Scandinavia by Viking and Arab traders. As well as dirhams, Viking hoards (left) often contain silver ingots or broken bits of jewelry, bowls, and jugs, ready for use in trade.

27

THE VIKINGS ARE COMING!

The *Anglo-Saxon Chronicle,* a history of Britain begun in the ninth century, tells that three ships sailed into an Anglo-Saxon harbor on the southern coast of England at the end of the eighth century. The local official of the king of Wessex, a man called Beaduheard, went down to the beach on horseback to speak to the sailors, thinking that they were merchants. They turned out to be Viking pirates, "sea-going pagans with roaming ships," who murdered Beaduheard and his companions.

LINDISFARNE

Another early, and much more famous, Viking raid took place in 793, on the island of Lindisfarne off northeast England. The monks of Lindisfarne were artists and craftsmen renowned for their beautiful bibles, prayer books, and chalices of gold and jewels. These the Vikings seized, after they had slain the helpless monks and burned their buildings.

RAIDERS AND LOOTERS

It was not only the British Isles that were at risk from raids. The Norwegians went west to Ireland and the Isle of Man. The Swedes turned their attention eastward, across the Baltic Sea to Russia and beyond, and the Danes sailed south to raid the Low Countries and northern France.

Their magnificent ships enabled the Vikings to voyage fast and far and to creep up unexpectedly on coastal settlements. They often captured the inhabitants and sold them as slaves. After each summer of raiding the Vikings returned home, their ships laden with booty. All along the coasts people kept a fearful watch for the dreaded longships and prayed that the Vikings would pass them by.

"In this year dire portents appeared and sorely frightened the people. They consisted of immense whirlwinds and flashes of lightning, and fiery dragons were seen flying in the air. A great famine immediately followed these signs and...on June 8th, the ravages of the heathen men miserably destroyed God's church on Lindisfarne with plunder and slaughter."
(Anglo-Saxon Chronicle)

A NEW PATTERN

After the first violent attacks, the pattern of raiding changed. Raids became more frequent and better organized. Even the great walled city of Paris was attacked several times by the Vikings.

> **The enemy was constantly bringing up fresh troops to reinforce the attack.... Stones smashed noisily onto painted shields. Bucklers groaned and helmets grated under the hail of arrows. Horsemen...threw themselves into the struggle.**
>
> — *Abbo of Fleury* —

It also became clear that many Vikings were not just attacking for treasure. Some colonized the fertile land along the coasts and rivers. They seized land in Frisia, on the Seine River, and the island of Walcheren. They began to till the soil and marry the local people. But even these expeditions were short-lived compared to the major campaigns to subdue England. In 865 a Viking "great army" spent the winter in East Anglia and then seized the city of York. Soon the Vikings ruled most of north and east England. They also established strongholds in Ireland and on the Isle of Man, where they remained until the twelfth and thirteenth centuries.

However, by the end of the ninth century, raids in Europe were already decreasing as defenses were improved and the Vikings were more often defeated in battle.

This beautiful manuscript was illuminated (painted) by monks in England in the eighth century. It was stolen in the ninth century by Viking raiders, but bought from them by an Anglo-Saxon ealdorman (an official responsible for local defense). He returned it to the Church at Canterbury.

REASONS FOR RAIDING

There were several reasons for the raids. Some raiders were outlaws from their homeland who had turned to piracy. Also, a shortage of agricultural land and the increasing power of the kings meant that many freemen and chieftains looked elsewhere for wealth — such as the lands and rich monasteries of Europe. And some chieftains were hired to fight other bands of Vikings, or to attack the hirer's political rivals.

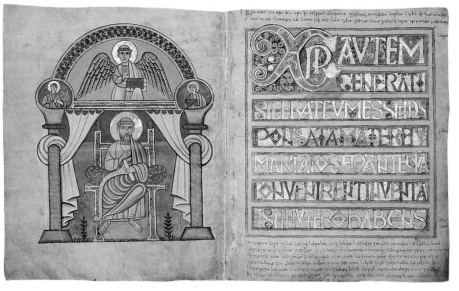

WEAPONS AND WARFARE

The ferocity of the Vikings in battle was legendary. Their superb ships gave them great mobility, and their enemies came to respect their bravery and cleverness in battle.

WEAPONS

Viking warriors took great pride in their weapons, especially their swords. Some soldiers were so fond of their swords that they gave them names, such as "Gold-hilt" or "Leg-biter."

Warriors also used spears, axes, and bows and arrows. There were two kinds of spear: a throwing spear and a thrusting spear. The first was used at the beginning of a battle, when a shower of spears was rained down on the enemy. The thrusting spear was used in hand-to-hand fighting — if the enemy had not already fled in terror at the sight of the advancing horde!

A sword was a Viking's most treasured possession. It was often beautifully decorated, sometimes with gold and silver. A Viking would usually leave his sword to his son.

A skirmish between a party of Vikings (left) and Frankish soldiers in the Carolingian Empire. Although they used horses for transport, the Vikings usually fought on foot. Here they have gathered behind a stream ready to face some Frankish cavalry.

BERSERKERS

Some warriors, called *berserkers* ("bear shirts"), were particularly feared. They howled very loudly as they fought in a mad rage, careless of their own safety. The berserkers thought of the bear as a kind of magical mascot. Because of this belief in magic, and their cruel behavior, they were outlawed when Scandinavia was converted to Christianity. Today we still use the phrase "gone berserk" to describe someone who loses self-control.

ARMOR

Only wealthy warriors could afford a coat of mail armor. Mail must have been very hot and heavy to wear. Wealthy soldiers also had iron helmets, some with nose and eye guards. Most warriors had just a leather cap and a brightly painted shield to protect them. Shields were round wooden boards, with a circular iron boss in the center to protect the hand.

Although the Vikings were ferocious in attack, chieftains might need to draw their men around them in a tight defensive formation with their shields overlapped. In the center would be the standard-bearer.

THE VARANGIAN GUARD

In the tenth and eleventh centuries, Vikings served as soldiers of the Byzantine Empire. At first they journeyed to Constantinople as mercenaries to fight wherever they might be sent. By about A.D. 1000 their reputation had grown so great that they were formed into the famous ax-bearing Varangian Guard, protecting the Byzantine emperor himself.

SHIPS IN BATTLE

The Vikings also fought from their ships. A saga tells of an attack on Old London Bridge by Olaf Haraldsson:

[The ships] rowed up under the bridge, laid their cables round the piles...and then rowed off as hard as they could downstream. The piles were thus shaken at the bottom and loosened under the bridge....The bridge gave way; a great part of the men upon it fell into the river, and all the others fled.

— St. Olaf's Saga —

Sometimes there were battles between huge fleets of ships, especially when Vikings fought Vikings. In these battles the defenders' ships were roped alongside each other. The chieftain's ship was at the center of this great platform. The attacking fleet then tried to board his floating fortress in the face of a hail of spears and arrows. Norway's King Olaf Tryggvason was killed at a great naval battle in about 1000 by his former allies, including Svein Forkbeard, the king of Denmark.

ROYAL FORTRESSES

A number of tenth-century Viking fortresses have been found in Denmark. Each has a circular bank with a ditch outside it, and entrances at the four points of the compass. The barrack buildings inside were made of wood and had curved walls and external buttresses, or supports.

The forts were probably built by Harald Bluetooth to control areas of countryside and important land routes, as were later medieval castles. They were part of a major improvement in defenses that took place during the tenth century.

The Vikings fought some fierce naval battles. The attacking force would try to board its opponent's ships and engage in hand-to-hand combat.

DEATH AND BURIAL

Some Viking warriors, especially in Russia, were cremated on huge funeral pyres. Often a slave girl was killed to accompany her master into the next world.

The Vikings believed in a life after death, and so people were buried with the things they would need in it. Food, drink, weapons, jewelry, dogs, and horses might be placed in the grave by the dead person's friends and relatives. Women might have pots and pans and some of the clothes they had embroidered or woven. These objects were also symbols of how wealthy and powerful the person had been.

MOUNDS AND GRAVES

The Arab traveler Ibn Fadlan observed Viking burial customs when visiting settlements along the Volga River. He wrote that when a chieftain died, he was put in a grave with many objects. A companion, probably a slave girl, was then strangled or stabbed and buried with him. It was believed she would travel with the man into the afterlife. There she would rejoice with him forever in Valhalla, the legendary hall of warriors killed in battle.

JOURNEY INTO DEATH

Wealthy Viking warriors might be buried in a ship or wagon because the Vikings thought of death as a journey. Most people had only a simple grave. A person who was not rich or important enough to be buried in a ship might have a grave marked by stones laid out in the shape of a boat (called a ship-setting).

ROYAL BURIALS

Kings, chieftains, and their families were buried in magnificent ships that had been dragged onto land. The richest Viking ship burial ever discovered is the Oseberg ship from about 850. The ship contained two women, one a queen, perhaps named Asa, and her slave, who was sacrificed in their tentlike chamber. The ship's timber had been preserved in its mound by the stones, clay, and peat sods heaped over it.

Items that could be used in a new life were buried with the dead. This bucket, decorated with small seated figures on the handle, was found in the Oseberg ship.

THE OSEBERG SHIP

1 Burial chamber
2 Tapestry
3 Kitchen utensils and
  other goods
4 Sacrificed ox

5 Ornately decorated
  carriage and sleds
6 Sacrificed horses
7 Mast
8 Mound being built up

A royal burial

The Oseberg ship was made of oak and had fifteen pairs of oars. It was not designed for the open sea. It seems, from the splendor of its decoration, to have been a royal barge for comfortable sailing in calm water. With it were found all sorts of beautiful objects, many decorated with intricate animal designs. There were a four-wheeled burial carriage, sleds, beds, kitchen utensils, and storage vessels, as well as many sacrificed animals. The remains of a woven tapestry were found inside the burial chamber. The scene depicted on it is probably from a Viking legend. It shows horse-drawn wagons and men wearing loose-fitting trousers worked in yellow, red, and black threads.

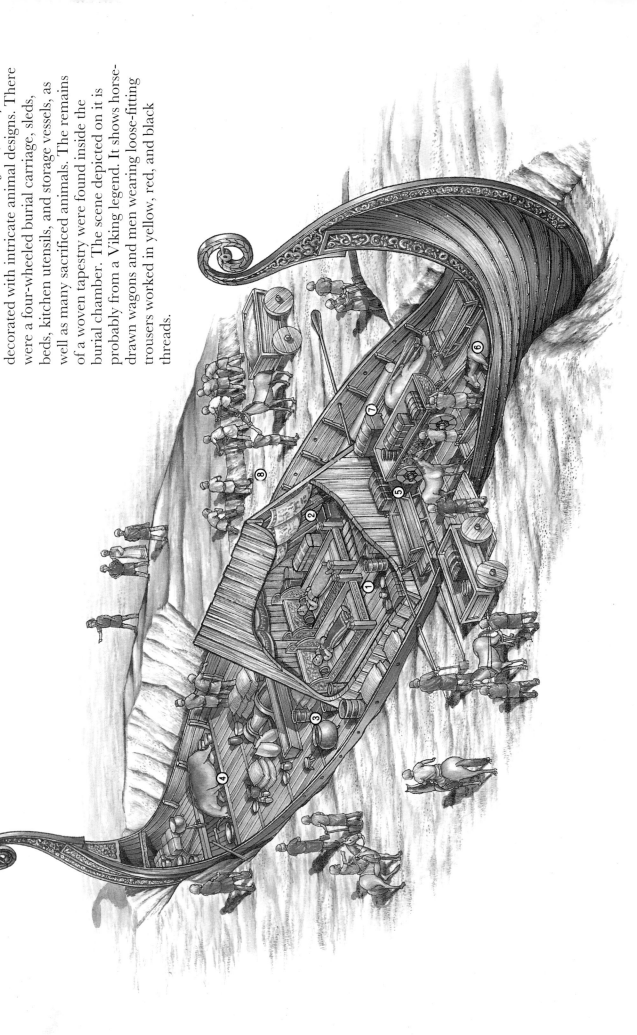

THE SETTLERS

The horror of the raids has echoed down the centuries and given the Vikings a very bad reputation. Yet many more Scandinavians traveled peacefully as settlers and traders.

GREAT VOYAGES

The Vikings' seaworthy ships and navigational skills enabled them to make remarkable journeys. They did not have sextants but probably had a primitive compass known as a bearing-dial. However, like other sailors of the ancient world, they could also find their way by looking at the moon, the stars, and the sun. At first the Vikings kept in sight of the land and came into the shore at night. As they became more confident navigators they sailed far out into the open seas, and even across the Atlantic Ocean.

PEACEFUL SETTLEMENT

The Vikings sailed to the Orkney and Shetland Isles in Scotland, possibly landing there before the raids began in earnest farther south. As well as raiding, many of these early settlers married women from the local culture, the Picts, and adopted their customs and styles of art. The Vikings also seized and settled the Isle of Man.

The monks and hermits of these northern isles were not as rich as those from the big monasteries farther south, and so the Vikings seem to have spared them. The Norse word for priest is "papa," and it survives today in the names of Orkney Islands, such as Papa Stronsay and Papa Westray, where hermits probably once lived.

ONWARD TO AMERICA

By 880 the Vikings had begun to settle in Iceland, and a century later they reached Greenland. Then, in 985, America was first sighted by a Norwegian called Bjarni Herjolfsson. He had set out from Iceland and had been sailing for three days when his crew lost sight of land.

Then their following wind failed and north winds and fog overtook them, so that they did not know where they were going. This continued over many days...before sighting land. Bjarni's men asked him if this was Greenland; he said he did not think so "for there were said to be huge glaciers in Greenland."

——— *The Greenland Saga* ———

Bjarni turned back, and it was the son of Eric the Red, Leif Ericsson, who had the honor of settling in North America. He gave names to the places where he landed: Helluland (land of stone), Markland (land of wood), and Vinland (land of vines, because of the grape vines that grew there).

This bronze ring pin was found by archaeologists at L'Anse aux Meadows in Newfoundland. The site had houses with turf walls, and may have been a Viking settlement.

The piece of wood below is probably part of a bearing-dial (shown below right). This simple instrument helped the Vikings sail great distances accurately.

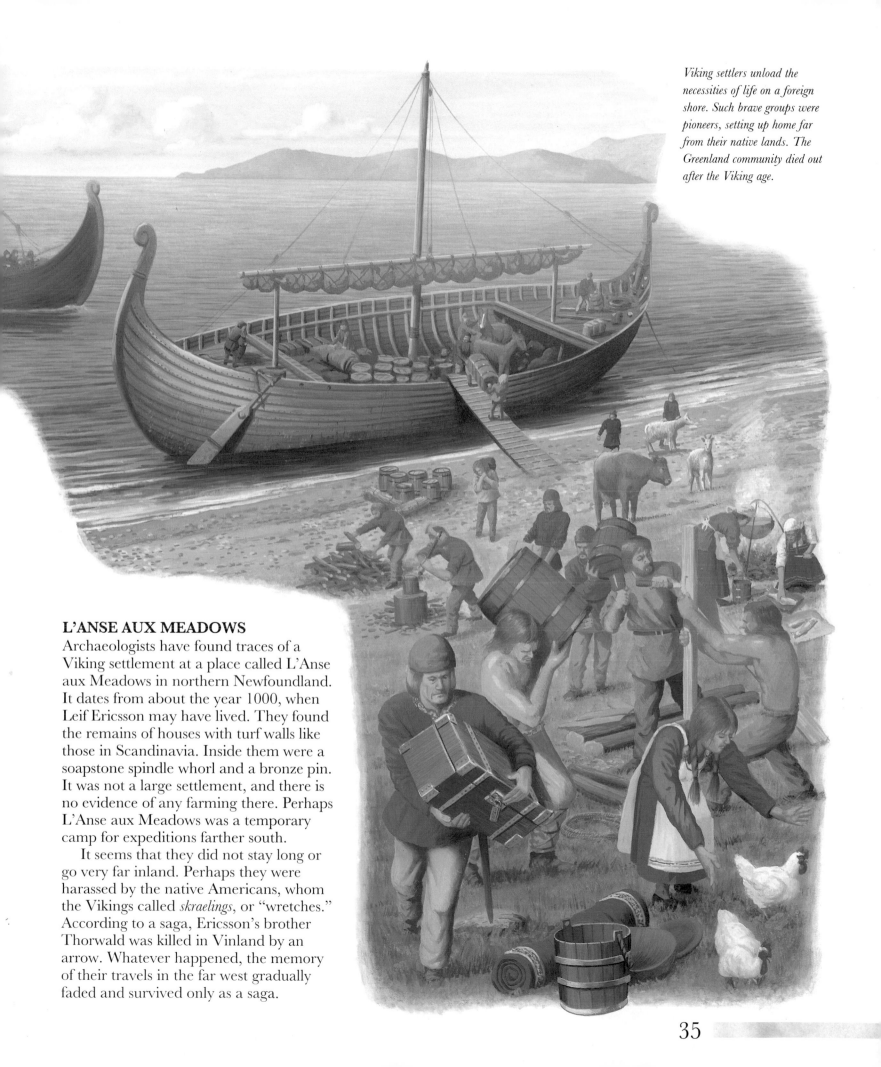

Viking settlers unload the necessities of life on a foreign shore. Such brave groups were pioneers, setting up home far from their native lands. The Greenland community died out after the Viking age.

L'ANSE AUX MEADOWS

Archaeologists have found traces of a Viking settlement at a place called L'Anse aux Meadows in northern Newfoundland. It dates from about the year 1000, when Leif Ericsson may have lived. They found the remains of houses with turf walls like those in Scandinavia. Inside them were a soapstone spindle whorl and a bronze pin. It was not a large settlement, and there is no evidence of any farming there. Perhaps L'Anse aux Meadows was a temporary camp for expeditions farther south.

It seems that they did not stay long or go very far inland. Perhaps they were harassed by the native Americans, whom the Vikings called *skraelings*, or "wretches." According to a saga, Ericsson's brother Thorwald was killed in Vinland by an arrow. Whatever happened, the memory of their travels in the far west gradually faded and survived only as a saga.

THE LAW

The Vikings had great respect for the law of the land. Those who did not obey the decisions of the Thing, the public assembly of all freemen, could be outlawed and put to death.

THE THING

Crimes were tried in court at the Thing, which made decisions about local government and acted as a court of law. Each national Thing met about twice a year, in spring and autumn, and lasted about a week. It was an important social occasion for the whole community, as people from the surrounding countryside came together. They caught up on the news, took part in games and celebrations, and bought and sold farm animals, tools, and craft objects.

People gather for a meeting of the Althing in Iceland. It was a time for games, conversation, and attempts to solve private feuds, before the formal discussions took place.

There were small local Things, which could meet at any time, and Things that served larger areas. In Iceland, which did not have a king, the *Althing* was the government of the whole country.

THE ALTHING

The Althing was held in midsummer at a place called Thingvellir ("Parliament Plains") in the southwest of Iceland. This was a huge open space surrounded by high cliffs that gave it very good acoustics.

The Althing lasted two weeks. It always opened on a Thursday, the day sacred to the god Thor, when the assembly was addressed by the chief priest. The law court was made up of thirty-six chieftains under the chairmanship of a lawspeaker. He was elected every three years and it was his job to recite the laws publicly.

A common form of ordeal for women was "caldron-taking." The woman had to put her hand to the bottom of a big vat of boiling water and retrieve some stones.

TRIAL BY ORDEAL

At a formal session of a Thing the accused were brought before a panel of neighbors and given the chance to prove their innocence. They might swear by the gods on a priest's ring, or call twelve men to swear to their innocence. Or they might undertake an ordeal, such as walking over red-hot iron. It was thought that the gods would protect the accused person from harm if he or she was innocent.

Although it was normal for people to speak for themselves in court, they could also use specialist lawyers, called lawmen. In some places, committees of such men, instead of the king, were responsible for drawing up laws. In England Danelaw, or "the law of the Danes," was established in areas under Viking control. When the English kings took over these areas they allowed the Vikings to follow their own, mainly Scandinavian, laws.

DUELS

Duels between two men were a method of solving disputes. The duelists had to stand in a clearly marked area, perhaps on a piece of cloth about two yards square, or surrounded by a rope on posts, like a boxing ring. If either of the fighters left the area he was regarded as a coward.

When blood was spilled the wounded contestant could bring an end to the duel by paying his opponent in silver. If one of them was killed, all his property went to the victor.

PUNISHMENT

The Vikings did not send a convicted person to prison. Criminals usually paid a fine. If they had injured someone they also had to pay the cost of looking after their victim. The fine for manslaughter was called *wergild* (man value) and was paid to the family of the deceased. For the worst crimes, such as certain kinds of murder, the criminal was outlawed and could be put to death.

Two men fight a duel. They must stay on the cloth and attack each other with their axes until one of them submits.

Odin rode an eight-legged horse called Sleipnir. Odin was accompanied by two ravens called Hugin (Mind) and Mugin (Memory), who were his news-gatherers in the world.

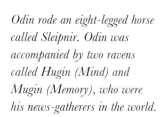

People often wore lucky charms in the shape of Thor's hammer. Many of these charms, as well as the molds for casting them, have been found.

For most of the Viking period the Vikings were pagan, worshipping many gods and goddesses. It was believed that these deities lived in a place called Asgard. There were also three Norns, sacred beings that represented the past, present, and future. The Norns spun out the destiny of gods and humans, which no one could avoid.

ODIN

Odin was the supreme god of Viking religion. He lived in his great palace of Valholl, or Valhalla, surrounded by a bodyguard of warriors who had been killed in battle. There they prepared for one last battle against evil that would end in Ragnarok, the destruction of the world. Odin was the all-powerful god of battle, wisdom, knowledge, and poetry.

THOR

Although Odin was the chief god, he was considered unreliable. Odin's son, Thor, was believed to be more predictable, and so was more widely worshipped by the Vikings. Thor was skillful in battle. He carried a mighty hammer, Mjollnir, which he used to destroy evil creatures. The Vikings believed that lightning was caused when Thor threw Mjollnir, and that thunder was the rumbling of his chariot. Yet Thor was thought to be a kind god, always ready to help sailors and farmers.

OTHER DEITIES

Other deities included Odin's wife, Frigg, his son Baldr, and the cunning and troublesome Loki. There were also Frey, the god of harvest and fertility, and his sister Freya, the goddess of love. A saga says of Frey: "He controls the rain and the sunshine and therefore the natural increase of the earth, and it is good to call upon him for the fruitful seasons and for peace." These gods were also worshipped by the Anglo-Saxons, and some of the gods' names survive as our days of the week: Wednesday was Odin's day or Woden's day, and Thursday was Thor's day.

RELIGIOUS CEREMONIES

The Viking religion did not have a separate priesthood, unlike the Christian Church and some other religions. Many chieftains acted as local religious leaders. Ceremonies took place in the open air, sometimes with feasting and sacrifice.

They hold a festival where they assemble to honor their god and eat and drink. Anyone who slaughters an animal by way of sacrifice has a pole outside his house door and hangs the sacrificed animal there.

— *Al-Tartushi* —

This scene is based on descriptions by Ibn Fadlan. He described how Vikings prayed to their gods in the open air. Here some merchants offer thanks for a safe voyage.

Although no Viking temples have survived, we know about one of them from a description by the Christian priest Adam of Bremen, in about 1070. He said there was a temple "entirely decked out with gold," where the people worshipped the gods and made sacrifices of human beings and animals in a wood close by.

Pagan ceremonies took place in sacred woods or by springs. There was probably a crude altar of stones. Some very realistic animal masks have been found. Perhaps these were worn when making sacrifices.

HUMAN SACRIFICE

A story tells of one particularly gruesome method of sacrifice. A cut was made down the victim's back, his rib cage was opened and his lungs pulled out and spread like an eagle's wings. Although this torture was probably invented by the storyteller, other methods of sacrifice, such as stabbing and strangulation, were no less horrible.

The imposing stone cross at Gosforth in Cumbria, England, shows the mingling of pagan and Christian beliefs. The Christian crucifixion is carved on one side. On the other side are scenes of Ragnarok.

A metalworker in Denmark obviously had both pagan and Christian customers. He made this soapstone mold from which he could cast both the Christian cross and the hammer of Thor.

From early in the Viking age, missionaries traveled to Scandinavia to convert the Vikings to Christianity. Although most of them were treated with tolerance, at first they were not very successful at spreading their faith.

EARLY CONVERTS

One of the first missionaries was the Englishman Willibrord, who in the early eighth century tried without success to convert the king of the Danes. Eventually Harald Bluetooth, king of Denmark, gave permission for preaching throughout his kingdom. Harald and Denmark were converted in about 960.

Scandinavians who had traveled abroad adopted Christianity much more readily. Merchants, diplomats, and settlers saw how wealthy and powerful the Christian rulers were, and thought that they had been rewarded by their god.

WEALTH AND CONVENIENCE

Some Vikings became faithful Christians through genuine belief. Others found it politically or financially convenient. Many merchants had to become Christians because the Church forbade any Christians to deal with the pagans who raided its lands and monasteries.

Kings were the most important converts. As well as trying to gain the support of its powerful god, they used Christianity to increase their own power. They benefited from improved relations with foreign rulers, while the new, centralized Church reduced the influence of local chieftains. In about 1000, King Olaf Tryggvason of Norway began a ruthless effort to strengthen his power and force his people to accept the Christian Church. Another king, Olaf Haraldsson, completed Norway's conversion to Christianity and was later made a saint.

The Church disliked the slave trade, particularly when Christians became the slaves of pagans. A story tells how a bishop was riding past some slaves. One of them cried out that she was a nun and started to sing a psalm. The bishop bought her freedom for the price of his horse and saddle.

THE ENDURANCE OF PAGANISM

In Iceland, the Althing, under pressure from the first Olaf, formally adopted Christianity in 1000. It was agreed that the people could still sacrifice to the old gods, provided they did so in private.

We are told that one Viking "believed in Christ and yet made vows to Thor for sea voyages or in tight corners, and for everything that struck him as of real importance." Many Vikings were still reluctant to abandon the old gods. Sweden remained pagan longest, well into the thirteenth century, even though pagan practices had been forbidden in 1100.

Stave churches

After Christianity was accepted, the Scandinavians took to church building on a big scale. In a very short time many hundreds of churches were erected. They were made of wood, as were most Scandinavian buildings until modern times. They were called stave churches because their walls were built of upright staves or planks with their ends sunk into the ground. In Denmark and Sweden such wooden churches are often found under existing ones. A few have survived only slightly altered, like the famous one at Borgund in Norway that dates from about 1150.

Timber post

Crosspiece

A STAVE CHURCH

1 Entrance porch
2 Tall frame
3 Upright planks, or staves
4 Wooden tiles
5 Decorative carving
6 Door
7 Bowl or font for Christian ceremony
8 Benches for congregation

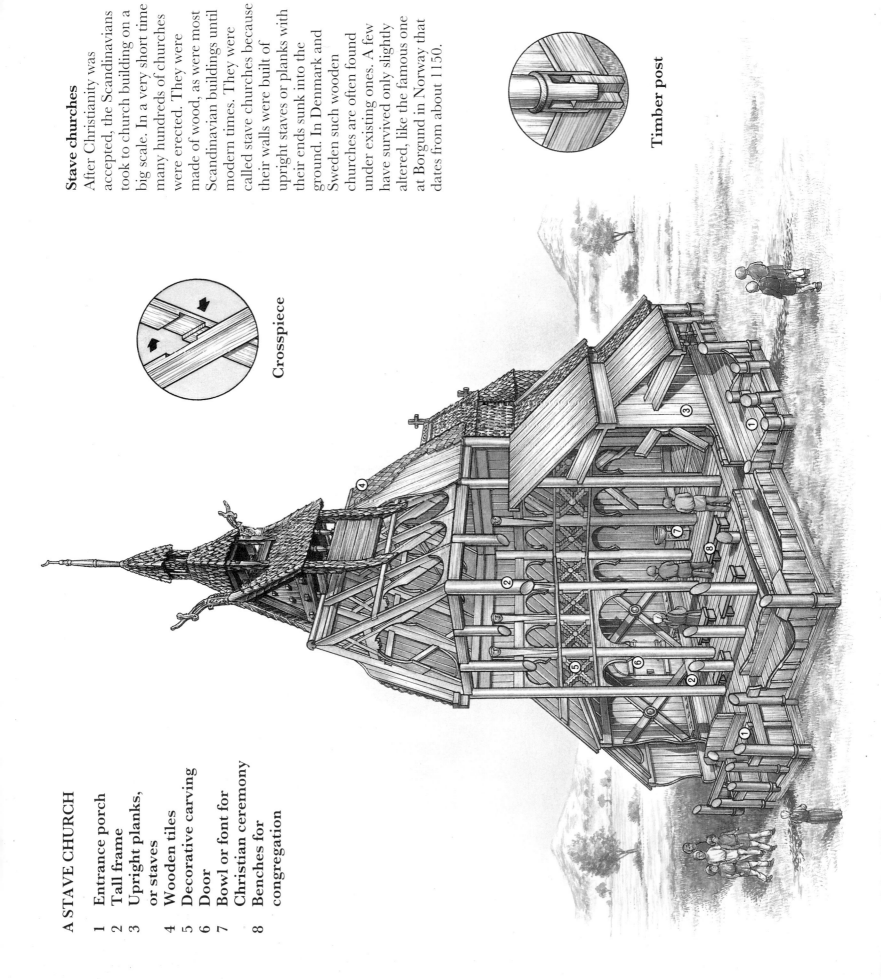

SAGAS AND RUNES

In the Viking age, the spoken word was more important than writing. Laws, religion, customs, and history were passed from generation to generation by word of mouth. Writing was limited to the use of the sticklike runes carved on bone, wood, stone, or metal.

The skalds were rewarded with valuable gifts, such as these silver arm rings, for composing new poems.

RUNES

The runic alphabet had sixteen characters. It was used before the introduction of the Roman alphabet we use today, and was called the *futhark* after its first letters, just as we call our alphabet the ABCs. The runes could be quite confusing because some of them had several meanings. On the other hand, they were easy to "write" down — as long as a person had a piece of wood and a knife for carving them! Runes have been found carved on many everyday Viking objects.

THE SKALDS

Skalds were court poets. They recited to the guests gathered around the fireside at the banquets held by Viking kings. Their long and intricate stories of gods, battles, and seafaring lasted into the early hours of the morning.

The skalds held an honored place in Viking society. They accompanied the kings and nobles into battle, so they could later sing of their deeds. Their poems and stories were handed down over the years, from generation to generation.

In about 983 King Harald Bluetooth set up a carved stone. This replica of it shows the figure of Christ on one side. An inscription on the stone reads that Harald "won for himself all Denmark and Norway, and made all the Danes Christians."

THE SAGAS

Many of the stories were written down from around 1200, after the end of the Viking age. They are known as the sagas. Some of the events in them are rather difficult to believe and have probably been exaggerated over the course of time.

Much of what we know about Viking royalty comes from these sagas. They are full of heroic tales of Viking gods, kings, and nobles. Famous ones include the *Poetic Edda*, *Egil's Saga*, *Njal's Saga*, and *The Saga of Olaf Tryggvason*.

The sixteen characters of the runic alphabet. The characters do not have horizontal lines, which could have been confused with the grain of the wood they were carved on.

f u p a r k h n i a s t b m l R
(th)

THE *POETIC EDDA*

The *Poetic Edda* is a collection of poems about the Vikings' gods and heroes. One of the poems is called *The Words of the High One*. It is a series of wise sayings, such as: "Look carefully around doorways before you walk in; you never know when an enemy might be there."

There is no better load a man can carry than much common sense; no worse a load than too much drink.

———— *The Words of the High One* ————

EGIL'S SAGA

This is a historical story written partly in prose and partly in verse. It tells of a great Viking warrior-poet called Egil Skallagrimsson, who probably lived in Iceland in the tenth century.

The following lines from *Egil's Saga* sum up the Vikings' love of adventure, battle, and seafaring:

**My mother once told me
She'd buy me a longship,
A handsome-oared vessel
To go sailing with the Vikings:
To stand at the stern-post
And steer a fine warship,
Then head back for harbor
And hew down some foemen.**

———— *Egil's Saga* ————

This saga and many others were written down by a Christian writer called Snorri Sturluson. Snorri lived in Iceland in the thirteenth century. He drew together many sagas that people still knew by heart, and he added to them some of the poetry of the skalds.

A skald enthralls his audience with tales of his king's courage in battle. The skald was probably with his king at the battle he is describing. Since the skalds were employed by kings and chieftains, they wrote poems, called skaldic poems, that usually praised their employers. Eddaic poems told stories about the gods or ancient heroes. The simpler rune poems, which are found carved mainly on rune stones, were brief poems that usually praised a local person.

This is the royal seal of the Norman king William I, who ruled England from 1066 until 1087.

A Viking chieftain is handed the keys to a French town. Perhaps the Vikings will protect the area from other raiders, or maybe a French noble is buying their support against his rival.

The Viking age came to an end after three centuries. By this time many Vikings were living in towns. They were now traders, not raiders, and their descendants in France, the Normans, began a new phase in the history of northwest Europe.

A QUIETER LIFE

Why did Viking power decline in Europe? Firstly, rulers in western Europe started to defeat them in battle more often, or made agreements with them. For example, in 911, King Charles III of France gave territory in Normandy to a Viking leader named Rollo. In return, Rollo became a Christian and promised to govern the region peacefully. Secondly, the influence of Christianity meant that the Vikings became less warlike. Finally, the valuable trade with the Arabs was disrupted by upheavals in the Middle East. However, the decline in Viking power did not happen overnight.

MORE VIKING INVASIONS

In the ninth century, Vikings had invaded and settled in north and east England. Only Alfred the Great, the Anglo-Saxon ruler of the southern kingdom of Wessex, had stopped them from conquering the whole country. By 954 his successors had thrown out the Viking kings, and Anglo-Saxon kings again ruled all of England.

Then, in the late tenth and early eleventh centuries, the Danes and Norwegians launched major new campaigns to subdue England. The Anglo-Saxon ruler Ethelred, known as "the Unready" because of his incompetence, tried to persuade the invaders to go away. He gave them huge sums of money, raised by a special tax called the *Danegeld*.

You must send treasure quickly in return for peace, and it will be better for you all to buy off an attack with treasure, rather than face men as fierce as us in battle. We need not destroy each other, if you are rich enough.

——————— *"The Battle of Maldon"* ———————

This picture shows Canute, with his wife, Emma, placing a jeweled cross on an altar. An angel is lifting the crown from Canute's head and pointing up at a figure of Christ, as if to say that all earthly power really comes from God.

VIKING RULE

This payment did not keep the Vikings away. They took the money but kept coming back. In one year alone, 994, the English had to hand over almost forty tons of silver. Eventually the Viking Svein Forkbeard forced Ethelred to flee to Normandy, and became king in his place.

In 1016, Svein's son Canute became ruler of England and, later, Denmark and Norway. Canute's power was recognized all over Europe. He was a strong and wise king, a Christian who went on pilgrimage to Rome and upheld the rule of law. Sadly, he died young in 1035. During the reigns of his less able sons, Canute's so-called "North Sea Empire" collapsed.

1066

England returned to Anglo-Saxon rule. Then, in 1066, the powerful Norwegian king Harald Hardrada invaded northern England. There he was defeated and killed by the English king Harold Godwinson at the Battle of Stamford Bridge, near York.

While Harold Godwinson was at Stamford Bridge, an army led by Duke William of Normandy landed in southern England. Harold, after one hard battle, had to march south to confront the new invader. He was defeated and killed at the Battle of Hastings by William, who became known as "the Conqueror."

THE VIKING AGE ENDS

The death of Harald Hardrada symbolized the end of the Viking age. Scandinavian power was no longer dominant in Europe, where a new medieval Christian world was developing. The Viking age of major seaborne raids, of heroic battles, duels, and Danegeld, was over.

And yet William's Normans were themselves the direct descendants of Rollo's Vikings who had been granted Normandy in 911. In a sense, then, the Norman conquest of Britain can be seen as the last great Viking invasion.

In a long and fierce battle at Hastings, the English king Harold Godwinson was defeated by the Norman army of William of Normandy. William then became king of England. He later put down several uprisings against him and defeated three Viking expeditions that tried to restore Viking rule to England.

KEY DATES AND GLOSSARY

The dates shown below relate mainly to Viking activity in Western Europe. The history of the Vikings in the East is poorly documented.

ca.650 Scandinavians from Sweden settle south and east coasts of Baltic Sea

793 Attack on Lindisfarne

795 First attacks on Ireland

ca.795 Vikings land in southern England

ca.800 Arab coins reach Scandinavia, contributing to the expansion of the Viking economy

804 King Godfred of Denmark attacks Charlemagne's Carolingian Empire

808 Hedeby founded

814 Charlemagne dies

820 Viking fleet raids French coast

835 Major Viking raids in Europe begin

841 Foundation of Dublin

843 Carolingian Empire divided. Vikings spend winter in Europe for first time

844 First recorded expedition to Spain. Moors defeat Vikings

845 Paris conquered

850 Vikings settle along Seine River

860 Viking expedition sails into Mediterranean Sea

ca.860 Rus come to power in Novgorod

865 Danish "great army" lands in England

866 "Great army" captures York

ca.875 First Vikings settle in Iceland

876 Settlement of England begins

ca.882 Rus come to power in Kiev

885–86 Siege of Paris

ca.890 Norway unified by Harald Finehair

892 Viking army, defeated in Europe, sails to England

911 Rollo given lands in Normandy

954 Eric Bloodaxe, last Viking king of York, killed

ca.975 Town of Birka abandoned

986 Expedition to Greenland

994 Olaf Tryggvason and Svein Forkbeard attack England

996 Birth of Canute "the Great"

1016 Canute becomes king of England and, in 1018, Denmark

1035 Death of Canute

1066 Battles of Stamford Bridge and Hastings. Destruction of Hedeby

1170 Dublin conquered by the Normans

13th century Sagas written down

Glossary

Althing: The national Thing, or public assembly, of Iceland, founded about 930

auroch: Now extinct wild ox or European bison

blood vengeance: A punishment of death inflicted by a relative of the victim

Carolingians: The family, including Charlemagne, that ruled lands of the Franks (in France and Germany) from the eighth to the tenth century

Danegeld: Tribute paid to Vikings to leave an area

Danelaw: "Law of the Danes," applied to parts of England that came under Viking rule, particularly after 876

Danevirke: Defensive earthworks in south Jutland

futhark: The Viking alphabet

gilded: Covered thinly with gold

hnefatafl: A board game like chess

martyrdom: Being killed because of a strong and persistent faith in a religion

mercenaries: Warriors hired to fight for a foreign ruler

pagan: Person who worships many gods

Ragnarok: "The Doom of the Gods," when the gods and warriors of Valhalla would fight a last battle against evil

ransom: Money or goods paid for the release of a prisoner

Rus: Vikings who went to Russia

skald: Court poet or storyteller

Slavs: A people living in eastern Europe

soapstone: Soft stone, smooth like soap, used to make cups and bowls

Thing: A Viking public assembly

tribute: Money or goods paid to ruler

Varangian guard: Viking warriors who served the Byzantine emperor

Quotations

The quotations in this book come from a number of sources. Adam of Bremen was an eleventh-century German bishop and historian who wrote *The Deeds of the Archbishops of Hamburg*. Adam never traveled in Norway and Sweden, but his work is an interesting history of Viking times as seen by a Christian bishop. The Muslim traveler Ibn Fadlan described in great detail the Rus he saw in Russia as he traveled along the Volga River in about 920. The descriptions of the raids on southern England and Lindisfarne come from *The Anglo-Saxon Chronicle*. This is a history of Britain begun in the reign of Alfred the Great (849–ca.900). The quote by Abbo of Fleury comes from his poem about the Viking siege of Paris in 885–86. Al-Tartushi was a Spanish Arab trader who visited Hedeby in the tenth century. The "Battle of Maldon" is an epic Anglo-Saxon poem about a great battle in 991, won by Olaf Tryggvason before he became king of Norway.

INDEX